# A GUIDE TO BEING OMG FABULOUS

How to get started when you realise you want more from life

**Melanie Gizzi**

© **Copyright Melanie Gizzi 2021 - All rights reserved.**
The content contained within this book may not be reproduced, duplicated or transmitted without direct written permission from the author or the publisher.

Under no circumstances will any blame or legal responsibility be held against the publisher, or author, for any damages, reparation, or monetary loss due to the information contained within this book. Either directly or indirectly. You are responsible for your own choices, actions, and results.

**Legal Notice:**
This book is copyright protected. This book is only for personal use. You cannot amend, distribute, sell, use, quote or paraphrase any part, or the content within this book, without the consent of the author or publisher.

**Disclaimer Notice:**
Please note the information contained within this document is for educational and entertainment purposes only. All effort has been executed to present accurate, up to date, and reliable, complete information. No warranties of any kind are declared or implied. Readers acknowledge that the author is not engaging in the rendering of legal, financial, medical or professional advice. The content within this book has been derived from various sources. Please consult a licensed professional before attempting any techniques outlined in this book.

By reading this document, the reader agrees that under no circumstances is the author responsible for any losses, direct or indirect, which are incurred as a result of the use of the information contained within this document, including, but not limited to, — errors, omissions, or inaccuracies.

ISBN: 9798768656522

## Dedication

Who am I doing this for?

I suppose anyone who is willing to spare their precious time to read it. So many women are asking for help but are unsure how to go from *thinking about* doing something to actually **doing it**.

If this can inspire you to take some form of action in the direction you want to go then I'll be over the moon and will have achieved my objective!

Of course, I am also doing this for my family, especially my children and grandchildren – to show them that if I can write a book, and learn to publish it myself, then anything is possible!

To my husband Heath, I love you more each day. I am so grateful for all that we have, and all of the love and support you provide for our family. I hope I can contribute as much as you have.

xxx

## CONTENTS

|   |   |   |
|---|---|---|
|   | A few words from others | vi |
|   | Introduction | Pg 1 |
| 1 | **O**nce Upon A Time | Pg 11 |
| 2 | **M**oments That Matter | Pg 22 |
| 3 | **G**etting Started | Pg 33 |
| 4 | **F**eel the Feelings | Pg 60 |
| 5 | **A**ction Taking | Pg 69 |
| 6 | **B**elief | Pg 84 |
|   | Conclusion | Pg 92 |
|   | Acknowledgements | Pg 106 |
|   | About Mel | Pg 111 |

## A few words from others

"Thank you so so much Mel. I can't put into words how much you have helped me. Don't ever doubt yourself, I am probably one of the most complicated case studies you will ever have and you have given me confidence to be me. To fit in and for once not give a flying fuck what others think. I will do what I want too, as long as it's constructive and kind. Not full of rage. Honestly that's huge for me. That proves you are the "magic mix", you will be successful and achieve your objective in helping people. Hurry up and get that book published please, you need to sprinkle your "magic mix" glitter far and wide and let others benefit like I have. Thank you, thank you, thank you xxxx"

— *Nikki Stephenson, Cheshire*

"Thank you for filling me with positivity you're such an inspiration so glad to have met you. You always have so much positive energy and always make me feel lovely. You help me to look at things differently which helps me to think at issues in a stronger way to sort them out head on. Thank you again." - *Tracey Williams, Conwy*

"You are my inspiration. If I could hug you I would. You have changed my life. Thank you from the bottom of my heart." – *Llinos Hughes, Denbighshire*

"Mel has helped me to completely change my life around for the better. Her support, inspirational personality and positivity makes you feel amazing, with Mel's encouragement I have lost over two and a half stone and feel FAB!"

– *Claire Stubbington, Denbighshire*

"Look at this – so chuffed Mel! Feel so much healthier! Drinks have definitely helped me to eat more mindfully and have given me a boost, also help me keep my water up. The support from the group has been amazing. So positive. I'm not sure I can be without the collagen now either – no more clicky bones! And hair and nails definitely stronger.

Also, I'm meditating and exercising more regularly and…I just signed up for a calligraphy course I have wanted to do forever and just never have! Honestly think this is all thanks to a shift in how I'm thinking about and prioritising things, thanks to you xxx" – *Carmel Smith, Conwy*

# Introduction

"I still don't know what I want to do when I grow up!". Is it normal to be saying that aged 38? Sat in the kitchen, inviting myself to take part in the conversation of my stepdaughter and her best friend. Two influential 21year olds, talking about their future prospects now their studies are coming to an end, a job interview is up for grabs and real life is on the cards.

That was me, March 2020, heavily pregnant. Watching our just turned two-year-old grandson Harley running around with our eight-year-old daughter Amelia, nursery and school both closed. Trying to fathom out what this pandemic was all about, thinking "What kind of a world is our son going to be being brought in to?".

Lockdown life pending. Little did we know just how crazy it would become.

With too much time on my hands, waiting for our new arrival, I started to think about the future. What life will be like when my maternity pay stops, how will I work? I can't do the same as before.

But then Freddy arrived and distracted my thoughts. We all had to 'stay home to save lives'. So that's what we did. A house bustling with five adults (the hubby Heath and I, the grown-up children of Heath & his first wife, Lesley, their daughter Emma, son Joe, plus his spouse Demi), the two little kids, a new-born and our dog, Grace.

In my new baby bubble, I put all worries of the future safely into a little box at the back of my mind. If only I could've thrown away the key.

As the months started to pass by it was almost like that well known board game (think Jumanji) was starting to rumble. Playing a sound in my mind, reminding me this was something I couldn't avoid. I was going to have to face the new way of life and make some decisions.

Going back to not knowing what I want to do when I grow up... it's a genuine feeling I've always had, and never been able to shake off. That feeling of not really being fulfilled. I wouldn't say I was unhappy, as I've loved the majority of my jobs, and am so grateful for all that we have. But something was missing. And I've found myself wondering many a time, if there is something more out there, and whether I am destined for bigger things.

Ellen Johnson Sirleaf said **"if your dreams don't scare you, they aren't big enough."**

I thought I had dreams or goals, but realistically, I never have. Nothing hard hitting, where I'm striving towards a massive achievement.

Don't get me wrong, I have achieved loads and I am really proud of all I've accomplished in my life to date. But what is the END goal? Where do I see myself when I'm on my death bed? What should I have accomplished by this time in my life?

Perhaps I was always too scared to think about it. In denial maybe. Or it could be that I thought I was too young to even need to think of the legacy I want to leave behind. Even in my high school Careers meetings I was unsure. An air hostess? A teacher? An interpreter? I couldn't decide. It frustrated me how so many of my friends seemed so clear, yet I was keeping my options open... Fast forward twenty years, and still no decision made.

Back in the days when I worked in Financial Services, I perhaps got close to teaching, being in the Learning and Development space. I remember being on a personal development course, one of many, since I've a thirst for knowledge (addicted maybe – she says rolling her eyes). When they posed the question "What do you want to be remembered for?" I knew straight away that I wanted to be known as 'A person who made a difference', cos that made me ***feel good***, but I just didn't know HOW?

Was this the start of me realising I needed to find my path? Perhaps.

At that time, I thought my path was paved out. Happy in the corporate world, in a well-established company, with a secure job. But of course, our circumstances change, and sometimes a light flashes along a different trajectory, catches our eye and screams out at us like a bright beacon to come this way. Or perhaps we find the decision taken out of our hands, and we are getting driven along down the wrong direction, either in silence, or kicking and screaming, but not being heard.

Life is a rollercoaster, don't you agree? I used to be petrified of them, rollercoasters. Until my bestie Nisha dragged me onto a ride in Busch Gardens. Holding my hand so tight she told me to keep my eyes open if I trusted her. Of course I do, with my whole heart. So, I did it. And it felt frickin amazing! Fear gone! Boom – just like that!

Something that had stopped me enjoying things in life for such a long time, was now no longer an issue. And all it took was a quick decision and a leap of faith. Magic!

Plus, it was a good job really, since six months from that date I had a tandem sky dive planned, which was of course to raise money for charity, Youth Federation. But also to help me conquer my fear of heights. However, on the day of the jump, since I'd already fixed that fear, I decided to not go for the originally planned 16,000-foot drop, and instead pay the extra twenty quid to go from 20,000 feet. "It's pointless paying for the videographer if you're going for the standard jump" said the instructor… "Fine then. Let's do it!"

Reflecting on this experience maybe helps prove to me that actually I do push myself at times. And can make spur of the moment decisions and take ownership for a situation. But it's taken a while to get there.

Being willing to step out of the comfort zone can be a step towards finding something that excites you or lights you up.

But how far out of that space are we willing to go. And what is it that holds us back?

Things change. Circumstances change. We change. It's all about how we adapt to these changes that determines the outcome. In part its choice, its mindset, its self-belief. Actually, it's definitely all of the above, and a bit more. Sometimes it comes down to skills and ability too, which means we have to develop ourselves.

So let's think of here and now.

At the end of the day if you're reading this, feeling a bit lost or flat, and unsure where life is taking you, and you actually want to be holding those reins and be clear on your destination then high five sister.... I've been in your shoes up until very recently. I found myself getting sick of just *thinking about* doing things, and actually wanted to start *doing them*. And that is why I've put pen to paper. I've been there, felt like that, and I'm doing this - I'm making things happen.

So, what even does OMG Fabulous mean?

Well, I hope that as you work through this book you will figure out what OMG Fabulous means for YOU!

This isn't one specific feeling that can be written on paper with a clear definition. Instead, it is that feeling where you experience that OMG moment, and you realise *what* it is that lights you up inside, it makes your heart feel full, and makes you want to do more of *that* thing.

And if you want things to change, you're going to have to dig deep. The severity of the change may be miniscule, but enough to make you feel fulfilled. And that's fab! But there is a chance that you may be in for a total overhaul, depending on what you uncover about your innermost desires.

It's going to take some self-discovery and perhaps you'll go as far as finding your vision and purpose. Then once it comes to you, you've got to hatch a plan to make it happen, don't let it go to waste.

Otherwise, you will always wonder "What if?", and you know I'm right.


One of the mantras I live by, and you'll see all over my socials is #sharingiscaring. And in more recent times #justdoit – thank you Nike! Why not share what we feel passionate about in order to help others. And why not just do it? Try new things, give it a go. What's the worst that can happen?


And now, we come back to the part of me wanting to be known as 'the person who made a difference'. Let me be that person for you.

Think of this short book as a chat with a pal. No judgement, no lecturing, just some handy hints on what you can start to explore if you're feeling in a place of uncertainty about your future. Like I said, that's where I was, I've been through this.

Becoming a self-development junkie, I've realised that a lot of the books and sources relay the same underlying messages, just in varying ways. And some resonate better than others.

I hope the things I highlight will land well and perhaps spark an OMG moment.

My wish for you is that you can take something practical away, to kick start the action needed to take you to where you want to be.

You're going to be given some questions at the end of each chapter which are designed to help you reflect on your journey so far, and to start to put some plans in place for the future. There is no right or wrong way to do this.

If journaling is new to you, I hope this will be an introduction that encourages you to continue getting the noise out of your head, onto paper. It is such a popular way to record our thoughts and feelings, not even necessarily to ever be revisited. Sometimes to make way for new ideas, increased creativity, or cope with stress and anxiety. The benefits listed are vast, and without a doubt it allows us to connect to ourselves at a deeper level. There was no question, I just HAD to include tasks as part of this book.

So please give it a go to get the most out of it. Grab a pen and let it flow. Look out for the Reflection Time at the end of each chapter. Download the workbook if easier (see back of book).

You may get to the end and realise you're happy just as you are, and if so that's great. At least you'll be confident in making a decision to do nothing. Because that's what it comes down to in the end, a decision.

We all have the power to choose the life we want to live.

We are all individual, and we were all placed on this planet for a reason.

Let's explore your purpose together.

We are only here once, make it count.

As author Kyle Gray said in his book 'Raise Your Vibration' **"The fact that you are here is a gift in itself, and anything you bring with you is a bonus"**.

## Chapter One

# Once Upon a Time

We all have a story. We all have a background, and experiences that have moulded us and brought us to our present day. And I'm afraid I'm not going to be able to tell you what it is that you're missing in your life. Only you are going to know that.

Do you feel stuck? If so, then you need to find a way to pull yourself out of the mud, get rid of the thing keeping you where you don't want to be or is holding you back. Perhaps you feel flat? If this is you, then it's time to think back to times where you felt lifted and at your best.

It might take quite a bit of delving to discover exactly what it is that's got you to this feeling you have right now.

It might take you days, weeks, months or years. Figuring out where your story changed or what beliefs have developed through your life will help you uncover what you may need to work on at the outset. There is even a possibility that you may not even get that far and may need help. But all of this activity comes down to self-care and self-awareness. If you're looking for a purpose or that missing thing you need to discover more about yourself. Perhaps it'll keep evolving as you keep developing yourself.

Yep, developing yourself.

That is the only way you are going to move forward and become unstuck.

So, I wanted to get that on the table right now, no surprises. I don't want you to get to the end and then realise you're going to have to actually do some stuff and make some changes in order to make things happen.

When I talk about developing yourself that can be small changes that cost you nothing, such as mindset and behaviour shifts. In comparison to something quite dramatic, where for example you may need to invest in yourself to develop your skills in order to achieve your goals.

But let's go back to...*how do you know when you're stuck?*

The dread of dragging yourself out of bed in the morning to go to that job that you no longer get excitement from. Or whatever the day is presenting you with that makes you want to hide.

Perhaps you've never actually been that excited about it, but it never bothered you in the past. (What are you doing? Get out! Ok sorry that's not practical!) But NOW for some reason it is bothering you.

Some people experience a lost feeling, like you're just not sure what your purpose is in life anymore.

Maybe you're approaching a big event. Perhaps a milestone age (like me) and you're thinking "holy shizzle am I seriously moving into my next decade?" and does this hold some kind of significance to the legacy you want to leave behind?

Perhaps you've recently experienced a big change in your life, such as a baby, a marriage, a divorce. A bereavement, redundancy, a new home, or just realising enough is enough. Any life changing event can be a trigger of more change to come.

We've all heard the phrase "new home, new baby" – by the way how much pressure does this put us under?!

Some things just aren't helpful are they! Especially not the stereotypical 'role' of a woman, which puts many of us under pressure.

Or should I say we put ourselves under pressure as we believe there is an expectation of us.

But going back to this example, of two major milestones to experience, and them arriving close together can be an absolute whirlwind. Some people will cope great, whilst others' lives will be turned upside down. A lot of it is down to our coping techniques, and of course our support network.

Experiencing big changes can actually give us more purpose, and more fulfilment. Personally, for me having my first child was an enormous but fabulous shock to the system. I didn't realise how life-changing it would be.

Becoming a Mummy was all I had wanted for years. I had been so fortunate to take on the role of step-mum, but it made me want to experience the baby years, which I hadn't had before. And it was magnified more so when I was told I would never likely conceive naturally, following a miscarriage, then an ectopic pregnancy resulting in a salpingectomy (removal of fallopian tube). That made the desire multiply by a thousand if not a million.

How dare someone take that possibility away from me?!

Incredibly just one round of IVF later, our first cycle, and our daughter Amelia was conceived. How amazing, we made this little human, and the first few days of her life she grew in a petri-dish in The Hewitt Centre of Liverpool Women's Hospital, before being put safely back inside Mummy (me) to carry for nine months, well, 36 weeks exactly to be precise.

Something changed when I gave birth to Amelia. Perhaps it changed earlier when the meds had switched off the pituitary gland in my brain that brings on the menopause. And had then flicked the switch back on to over-stimulate my ovaries and create lots of eggs. Add Ovarian hyperstimulation syndrome thrown into the mix to keep things interesting.

But her arrival definitely changed me, she became my priority over all-else.

Hormones can wreak havoc with our thought process can't they. For many women they play lots of tricks on us. Muddying the water, impacting our decision-making tool (our brain) by fogging things up and making things seem more difficult than they need to be.

This can be a regularly occurring issue for many women, and no matter how many supplements we introduce there may still be the monthly dread of "that time" where we struggle to control the emotions, even rages, the choices and somehow everything becomes justified by our thought process of *this is just how I am*.

Why do we do that? It's almost a submissive thing where we conform and let our barriers down. And this isn't just with hormones, there are so many other scenarios where we accept things because it's easier, perhaps expected (going back to the stereotyping).

But actually, it shouldn't be that way, and it doesn't need to be.

Luckily my TOTM has never been that bad, just the bloating and the ridiculous desire to eat anything sweet. Three sessions with a hypnotherapist to control my binge eating, and I've sometimes mastered the "fat off" mantra she introduced, but other times I just enjoy the choccy too much.

And that's life. We shouldn't strive for perfection, but instead balance and moderation.

I'm not saying that everyone should try to change or have therapy to combat any issues. But many people do try, for a time. Or they attempt to build new habits and if there is a bit too much effort required, or a lack of clear meaningful goal in place, then they give up.

What is really apparent to me is that so many of us just tend to accept things, and let things, possibly the easier or stereotypical route, become the norm.

Our expectations alter, and eventually we just go through the motions of the same old thing day in day out. Or in the example of what's just been mentioned, month in month out, and it's like we become accepting of our situations and that becomes our reality. Until one day we realise *I don't want to live like this anymore, and things have got to change.*

That realisation may come from the trigger event. As I mentioned motherhood was a big change for me. But the actual kick up the arse came in 2016, at the sudden loss of a friend. Gemma went out for a run and sadly never came home. Her heart stopped. At 34 years young, leaving behind three young boys and a husband. Taken far too soon.

Gem's departure made me stop and think. A month younger than me, we had similar fitness levels, both liked to run. She always seemed so happy and had a real zest for life. And the most beautiful smile which I can still see. She runs alongside me when I jog now, a psychic told me. Reminding me with gusts of wind when I ask her for help.

Her passing made me realise that we truly never know when our day will come. It sounds cliché but life IS for living, and we owe it to ourselves to live our best lives. I wasn't aware of it at the time, but on reflection I have a lot to thank Gemma for. I started to take ownership for my life and make radical decisions. I'd never done that before. Pushing myself further out of my comfort zone became a more frequent thing. I left my secure and stable corporate job, despite being successful in a promotion, and the leaps of faith started to get bigger.

Being OMG Fabulous is NOT about feeling stuck in a situation where you've just accepted life the way it is…

**Mel's Mantra:**

**Opportunities exist around us.**

**Move forward or stand still.**

**You have the power to share your Glory**

Reflection time: OPENNESS

What do I want to change?

Future thinking: Why? What difference will it make?

## Chapter Two

# Moments That Matter

So, you've had the thought or maybe you've even been brave enough to say it out loud *"I don't want to live like this anymore, and things have got to change."*

Let's pretend you're the person who has just experienced a life-changing scenario, a trigger. And let's categorise these triggers into two types. Those which bring us joy, and those which bring us heartache. Dependent on the category you fall into there may be some questions that start to pop into your head every now and again, or perhaps constantly…questions such as:

*What's next?*

*What am I supposed to do now?*

*How do I get through this?*

*Is this even real?*

At times you will try to answer those questions, and you might do a pretty good job of having a chat with yourself and coming to some kind of conclusion. But the next day you might be faced with the same question, and the answer is no longer there. Nothing presents itself.

## Mindset

Our minds can be consumed with totally different things at any given time depending on where our emotional state is at. How we answer these questions, and our inner talk can all be a varying tone, depending upon what we are thinking and how we are feeling internally. That's why it is SO important that we invest in ourselves.

As they say, "you can't pour from an empty cup". And what I mean is to realise your self-worth. Realise how significant YOU are in this world. If you don't love yourself, how can you expect others to love you.

Treat yourself as you would treat your best friend, and talk to yourself in the same way.

Mindset is quite possibly the most important factor in where you go from here.

We can think about our mindset as the way in which we communicate with ourselves. That's pretty big isn't it.

So basically, what we believe, we think. And what we think is what we tell ourselves, which will ultimately lead to some kind of action or decision making.

Using the mind positively and productively is essential in moving forward from a situation. Being attuned to emotions such as empathy and compassion allow us to connect with others at a deeper level, with more meaning and purpose.

In times of adversity, we often need or seek those qualities in others, and can learn from the way in which others treat us. Being able to show kindness and respect for those around us builds trust. Having strong relationships can help us feel a sense of security, warmth, belonging and peace.

I feel so blessed to have had such a stable and secure upbringing. I don't really have any hard-hitting stories of an awful childhood that I've survived. Being bullied in high school wasn't great of course, but it could have been worse. I had a great group of friends. Charlotte still being one of my closest 30 years on, and still in touch with many others.

My parents are the most supportive, loving and inspirational human beings that I know. I have so much to thank them for. I truly believe my brother Joe and I can thank our folks for many of our attributes and qualities.

We learn a lot of habits from those we are close to don't we. But we can also be influenced by other sources along the way. Whether it's getting in with the 'wrong crowd', or it may be that we are just trying to figure out who we are and discover what makes us tick.

I know I'm far from perfect, but my past makes me who I am today. It's shaped me and has brought me to this present day. I accept all my decisions, good and bad.

I believe life experience can teach us many skills without even realising.

Emotional intelligence doesn't come easy to everyone.

And like any skill it may need to be worked upon. Therefore, developing the soft skills that help us to effectively communicate with others will also help us to learn how to communicate with ourselves. And seeing all of the things we've experienced in life as part of OUR journey, we can actually call on these memories, the feelings and emotions to empathise meaningfully and help others too.

I'll share my example of what brought me to this point. It doesn't need to be thought of as negative. It's actually the best story I could tell! But I'll do the short version.

I was told I would unlikely get pregnant naturally. We had our daughter via IVF as mentioned in Chapter One.

Two subsequent cycles (Frozen Embryo Transfers), resulting in no babies. No birth control for ten years, a whole load of false alarms. Annual trips to see various clairvoyants or psychics, who each would tell me I'll "have a girl, then a boy" on every visit, gave me hope. And I never let go of this.

During my last visit to Jan Hurst, a clairvoyant from Rhos-on Sea, I was told to let nature take its course, a message from Winifred, my Nain (that's Welsh for Grandmother by the way) Mum's mum, who had never come through to me in a reading before. I was shocked but pleased to hear from her. She said IVF would put too much strain on us emotionally and financially. I agreed to be honest. So, we listened, and decided on no more fertility treatment.

I kept that visualisation of our boy in my arms. Even Nisha was told she would soon be holding a boy of someone so close to her. She rang and told me straight away. My boy?

Two months after I saw Jan, we discovered we were pregnant, au naturel! How flippin fabulous is that?!

Heath's 50th birthday party was successful shall we say!? Hee hee!

Our son Freddy was born April 2020, right at the start of the pandemic. The most magical miracle we could have hoped for, after our first blessing of fertility treatment giving us Amelia of course. I suppose this felt even more miraculous!

Both of us self-employed with no savings left, and unprepared for this miracle baby, we had to adapt to our new life. Maternity leave came to an end, and the "What's next?" question popped up too many times. Often resulting in tears.

Life wasn't going to ever be the same again, with additional responsibilities. But having our boy was all I wanted. He was the missing piece of our family puzzle.

Having Freddy has been another trigger. It has opened my eyes to a new way of living.

I have discovered things and a system which allows me to also be present, as well as work. Continue to progress personally and professionally, all whilst bringing up our children, which is my driver, my reason WHY – what's yours? (that'll be covered later).

Now let's think of this present day. What is the story you are telling yourself?

How are you playing this scenario out in your mind right now? Think of your future and how you may like to visualise yourself.

I expect you're doing one of two things right now…

You're either sitting there, reading this with a smile on your face, as you're picturing being sat poolside at your private villa in Ibiza (that's where my head is at right now, along with the goofy smile, and a glass of pina colada in hand).

Or you're in a state of panic. Your stomach is in knots and you feel dread as the image that falls into your mind is dull, grey, gloomy and sad.

If you're in the latter frame of mind can I ask to you to go back and re-read the question I asked.

*'Think of your future and how you may **like** to visualise yourself.'*

Let me be more direct. If there were no limitations where do you see your future self? What would your most 'perfect' life look like?

And I don't mean a life of insta-ready perfection. The one that puts so many people under tonnes of pressure as they believe that's what the outside world depicts as the 'ideal'. I mean the life that brings YOU the most joy. Where you can **F**eel, **A**ct, **B**e and have anything you want. Living your most authentic life, doing what makes you happy as your *most fabulous* version of yourself.

The power is in YOUR hands to think positively. Surely you don't want to be visualising a depressing future state. You are in the driving seat of your mind. You can choose how you **F**eel. Your thoughts, your visions, your aspirations will ultimately determine where you go from here. Taking inspired **A**ction is a real thing, and when you tune in to what you truly desire, you become your own inspiration and start to **B**elieve in yourself!

By writing it down you face the situation you are in. I hope that you realise that there is actually so much to be grateful for and life isn't as bad as you perhaps originally thought. But if it's a shit storm then let's thrash it out together!

Go wild now... if you need to carry on then grab more paper or go to the back of the book.

## Mel's Mantra:
## <u>O</u>ptimism <u>M</u>anifests <u>G</u>ood-feelings

Reflection time: MINDSET & MOTIVATION

What are my triggers? Why am I here?

Future thinking: If there were no limitations this is how my life would be… (write it out now)

## Chapter Three

# Getting Started

I hope you're feeling some kind of excitement by now?

Let's consider the kind of person you are. Are you the type of person who comes in with an "I can't" approach? Or the person who says "How can I?"?

How long ago was it since you last did some personal development?

Many people think that when they leave education they also leave behind the requirement to develop. This couldn't be further from the truth. No one knows everything, and we can continuously develop our minds intellectually, emotionally and mentally, in order to keep up with day-to-day life, but also to progress with our desires, and achieve more from life.

I will not apologise for using the phrase "*every day is a school day!*" (Picture the cheesy grin while I'm saying it, and my thumbs up!) I challenge you to learn something new, every single day!

If you read the description, 'A Guide to Being OMG Fabulous' is basically a helping hand when looking for **your own version of fulfilment.** You may be on the fence and undecided if you're classing yourself as unfulfilled. Maybe you're just a bit fed up. However you're feeling I hope this will help. So, let's get practical.

What is it that inspires you? Think about what fills your heart. It could be an activity, a subject or topic that you just can't get enough of.

What are your passions or hobbies? What is it that makes you feel motivated? Cast your mind back to a time when you felt so engrossed with a subject you just wanted to keep hearing more.

Perhaps there is something that you could talk about all day long. Is there a memory of you relaying information you heard to someone else?

Do you have a vision in your mind of something you've always wanted to achieve? Perhaps it was to become a personal trainer with your own gym. Or maybe you've always wanted to have your own beauty salon. Maybe you want to become a professional photographer or an author. Maybe you finally want to pass your driving test. Or go travelling?

Often, we find ourselves stuck and afraid to make a move, or to deviate from what we know because we are secure and safe in this place. But every now and again we may dabble with bravery and take a leap of faith closer to where we want to be. For example, enrolling on a course to develop our knowledge and skills.

To have the confidence to do this we may need to consider a few things:

What is it that I need or want to develop or learn?

Where can I get this support?

How much will it cost?

What if I don't do it? (If the thought of not doing it makes you feel disappointed, take note! Our 'gut feeling' is a real thing, it's telling us something and it shouldn't be ignored).

**Personal Development**

There are so many resources out there to aid personal development.

Take self-help books, like this one (Yes - I am doing this, I am putting myself in the self-help space eeeek!).

This may just be a quick fix to encourage you to want to do more. I hope it serves that purpose in getting you started, if ***more from life*** is what you want.

My life-changing read was *'The Miracle Morning'* by Hal Elrod.

I'd finished my first draft of this book on day 90. Second draft on day 160. As this goes to publish, I'm on day 265 of the Miracle Morning. The book comes with a 30day Challenge to encourage new habits. As you can see, I'm definitely bought in!

I believe my own version of my miracle morning routine – Hal gives the Life S.A.V.E.R.S – my version can be made into OMGFAB…

| | |
|---|---|
| **O**rganisation | **F**eel-in |
| **M**ovement | **A**ffirmations |
| **G**ratitude & Journaling | **B**reathing |

I followed the Life S.A.V.E.R.S to get me going and this is how it has evolved for me, and I didn't even realise until I was writing this book! It came to me after a meditation, just before I pressed PUBLISH! Cue last minute alterations (I am a deadline dancer that's for sure). But when the creative downloads arrive, don't ignore them! They're presented to you for a reason. Embrace the ideas. The more you pay attention the more they flow.

I highly recommend reading The Miracle Morning!!!!!

I read the book and when starting to journal I wrote down that I wanted to write my own book by the time I turn 40. Where on Earth did that come from? It just flowed out of me onto the paper. I told my husband and my parents but no one else.

I had no clue where to start or how to get going but I trusted the process. I know that the universe has my back, that might sound all woo-woo but it's a belief I now strongly have. (And I'm a fan of the woo by the way!)

Having a morning ritual (I used to call it "routine", but Niki Kinsella introduced the concept of ritual, as it's something we choose to do that benefits us – I love it! Thank you Niki) this morning ritual will be with me until I take my last breath. I allow myself a day off every now and again, that is fine. No self-punishment.

But in the main it's how I start my day.

Never before have I found a way to discover personal development time that allows me to be consistent in focusing on me and my goals. Its only during this time that I have now discovered how I can bring my purpose to life.

I have become inspired by my own journey, motivated by my 'WHY', my family. And here I am making it happen. Perhaps I want to prove it to myself too.

To see this through to completion will be magical.

I, little old me, have written this book that you hold in your hands, or on your electronic device, or perhaps I'm even talking to you in your headphones.

And it all started with an idea.


Invest in yourself.

Some changes we may decide to make, may only be small, but make all the impact that we need to get to our desired outcome. However other changes may be significant with monetary value attached. Therefore, your belief in your journey and destination is essential.

Whether your mode of development is a book, a course, a qualification or investing in a mentor or a coach, explore your options and keep an open mind. Never underestimate the power of connecting with someone who can help you find your self-belief and bring out **your fabulousness**!

You must know that YOU are worthy of this, and that you deserve the life you visualise.

Get those pictures in your mind and find the hard copy images to print off. How about making a vision board? Christine Kane's guidance helped me build mine, and it hangs on the wall in my office, for me to explore every morning as part of my morning ritual before and after I meditate. If you can feel it in your heart, see in in your mind, you can bring that reality to life.

It may be a requirement to change some habits or behaviours in order to move forward.

These can be physical habits, such as your wakey wakey time, or retraining your thought process, which we've already touched on. Your success in changing those again comes down to you. Some things will be easier than others depending how engrained they are. What you tell yourself about your success in this area, will be your reality.

***"Whether you think you can or you can't you're right"*** - Jim Rohn

**The Law of Attraction**

I can't believe I've managed to get to Chapter Three and this is the first time I'm mentioning The Law of Attraction (LOA). I wrongly assume that everyone knows about the LOA, so just in case you don't, the simplest way to explain it is to say that thoughts become things.

What we think about we attract into our lives.

There are hundreds of books on this. I AM A BELIEVER and FAN! I could write a whole other book on my own experiences of the LOA (maybe I will). But for now you'll just see a few dotted through this one.

I was first introduced to the LOA in 2013, in the book *'The Secret'* by Rhonda Byrne. This was the first time a book changed my life!

Considering the powerful impact that it had on me, I didn't do a very good job of continuing to **read** to increase my knowledge.

I was however really blown away by Byrne's book, and wanted the trilogy. But I was working full time and "I couldn't read because it would send me to sleep". That's what I always told myself, so of course that was my reality.

Instead, I bought the film 'The Secret' on DVD and purchased 'The Power' as a CD audiobook for my car.

A short time later I bought 'The Magic' paperback. That's a 28day practice of gratitude. But alas it's a habit and I told myself "I don't read" so I gave up, and I never got passed day nine. Twice.

Until this year when I told myself I was going to read the book in February to coincide with the days of the month, perfect.

I had read about habit formation in 'The Miracle Morning' and had a newfound belief that **I could read**, and get to the end, and I did. And it felt great!

So, I've touched on two key things in helping with your mindset – personal development and the Law of Attraction. But in order to get started, we do need to take action. And not knowing where to start can be the hardest part.

And then there are other considerations we sometimes

create in our minds and then welcome them as objections. And so we continue to sit there procrastinating. Such as finding the time…

Let's start with O for Organisation ☺

## Organisation

You may be thinking about your lack of time to even start to think about what it is that you want to change or are missing in your life. I was the same. Our minds are so consumed with the day-to-day life, and all the noise of the stresses we put on ourselves that we often don't allow ourselves time to think.

We need to carve out a period in the day for some "me time".

When? How? So, let's think about the stages of the day.

When you wake up every morning and when you go to sleep every night, are the two most important times of the day to influence your mind. Put that phone down, unless you're using it to listen to a guided meditation or an audiobook of course. So, one of these two time slots is going to be the best place to start.

The morning is the optimum time, so that we don't run the risk of being too tired in the evening and make an excuse that we will try to start again tomorrow.

Plus, we all know that how you start the day can set you up for success!

But you do need to find what works for YOU, because this is all about you!

Generally, people have their work commitments between the hours of 9am-5pm, or thereabouts. Or at least some set hours of the day where they're occupied, with no wiggle-room. Or perhaps if you're a parent you have commitments of little people 24 hours a day as well, dependent upon the age of your children. So how an earth do we find time to fit things in?

It starts with a decision.

YOU choose to decide that you are worthy of some time to yourself, and YOU allow that to happen in your life.

'Time' has got to be the biggest objection out there for most things. "I don't have enough time" is all I seem to hear. I used to use this phrase a lot too, before I started time-blocking, using my daily planner, and seeing how I actually use my time during the day. (Check out my 'OMG I am Organised' Daily Planner on Amazon by the way – now published - nudge nudge wink wink!)

**"You will never 'find' time for anything. If you want time, you must make it."** - *Charles Buxton*

The reality of it is that we all have the same 24hours in a day.

Granted some have a lot more commitments than others, but again it's up to you how you choose how you fill it.

If you want anything to change then you're going to have to **start being kind to yourself** and allow yourself a regular interval where you can concentrate on what's going on inside.

This is the starting point for self-care. And like all those social media posts say: "**Self-care is not selfish, it's essential!**".

I absolutely love that society is recognising more than ever, that we should be focusing on doing things that make us feel good, and also serve us well.

Awareness of how we spend our time is important. As then we can decide what stays and what goes, what we need more of and what we need to minimise.

I'm not sure of the original source but I love the quote "**A healthy outside starts on the inside**". For me this encompasses MY own ultimate wellbeing goal, which is *feeling fab on the inside and out*. How do you read it? I hope you'll take some time to ponder on this.

When we can love ourselves enough to prioritise "me time" on our To-Do list, we can connect on a deeper level with our true passions and even our purpose. Download my FREE Six Steps to Self-Care (link at the back of book).

**Movement**

Exercise has been a big part of my life since I started running in 2014 to raise money for Great Ormond St Hospital. Emma my stepdaughter was under their care since her toddler years through to adulthood. An amazing institution, who we will be forever grateful for. Em has never been held back, and excels at all she does, her health is now good and she is super fit. I've realised exercise has become an essential part of self-care for me and my own health too.

Isn't fundraising a great example of when we are willing to push ourselves out of our comfort zone for the benefit of others.

We know it results in the sponsorships, so we don't want to fail or let anyone down by not following through with our commitments.

Accountability can make all the difference when it comes to motivation!

As well as this, on most occasions, we do actually usually benefit too. E.g., committing to a half marathon when you don't usually run, increases your overall fitness, helps us find more energy, great sense of satisfaction upon completion too.

This also increases self-belief. As well as the support we give to charity, this can motivate us to keep going.


Our mind and body are two parts of one whole being. Being in good health can impact the mind, and vice versa. Its arguable that a healthy mind is more important as that can determine our level of motivation when deciding to lace those trainers up or roll out the yoga mat (check out Yoga Burn on the socials, Zoe is a wonderful teacher from starter to experienced). Yoga has really changed so much for me. I highly recommend it!

Adding some form of daily exercise into your routine not only releases the endorphins that help us feel lifted in mood and energy levels.

It of course has the physical benefits for your body too, such as helping with weight control, and risk reduction of serious illnesses. We also get a better night sleep which is essential for repair and restoration. And there is also loads of fun to be had!

The first bit, of getting started is the hardest. Take baby steps and set small targets. Aiming to move more every day. Even if it's parking further away from the shops, school or work.

If doing exercise does not float your boat, then why not consider the fundraising approach, or some kind of public commitment.

If doing it for someone else is the only way to get you started, then why not try? Put yourself out there with a goal and a deadline to drive the positive change within you and take a step forward.

The rewards will be mahoosive!


**Gratitude & Journaling**

Gratitude is such a powerful tool which opens your eyes to all the things here in your life today, that we can be absolutely grateful for.

We opened our eyes this morning, we are alive. That's a good place to start!

Try waking up every day and thinking of at least three things, ten if you can, to be grateful for. Do the same before bed.

This activity leaves it pretty much impossible for you to wake up or go to sleep in a bad mood.

It also encourages mindfulness, appreciating what we have in our lives right now and that where we are is exactly where we are supposed to be. This is all part of a process.

Amelia and I use a gratitude stone, a rose quartz crystal, every night before bed to talk about what we are most grateful for from the day. This is practiced far and wide, in different variations. For us it's a beautiful ritual, and a special moment that I really treasure, and I know she does too.

Long may it continue!

(There are so many journals and workbooks leaning towards these type of activities for kids, it's awesome!)

It's even more powerful when you write down what you are

thankful for.

Ever kept a diary? I did as a teen, but nothing more than a daily to-do list in more recent years.

However now, with my daily planner, and journaling, I have created a space for gratitude. This takes things to a whole different level, and I see the difference that it has made in my life already.

Through the activities in this book, I am offering you the chance to journal your thoughts. The power of getting everything out of your head and on to paper is immense, it's so therapeutic.

There is no right or wrong way to do it. Some of my most creative moments and thoughts come to me when I'm taking that time in the morning to focus on me, my thoughts, my feelings, my aspirations for the day ahead.

Let your thoughts go, and let the words flow. There is no right or wrong way to journal, but plenty of tips online.

**Feel-in**

What an earth does this mean? Well, I'm not gonna lie, I

needed an F! LOL! And the whole next chapter is called Feel the Feelings – this is what it's all about, how we feel.

But I want to put it in as a reminder in terms of Getting Started – **tune in to how you feel, always**. What makes you feel good or crappy, so there is association with your actions, and you can choose more of the good stuff! Awareness of how you feel can alter your choices next time, and reduce those sabotaging moments too.

**Affirmations**

Affirmations can hold real significance in encouraging self-belief. Again, going back to '***whatever you tell yourself becomes your reality'***.

You can be in control of your affirmations, and/or use prompts or tools to help you out.

There are various ways to do this. Some people shout things at themselves when working out. Picture "C'mon your legs are strong, you can do it" while you're running up a hill!

Or self-talk in a mirror before an interview "You've got this!". That's the same principle.

But writing down affirmations, as the person you see yourself becoming, and **feeling** it as though it has already been achieved, can really alter your mindset.

There may be one, or a list of affirmations that you stick to for a certain amount of time. Or perhaps you want to start with a fresh set depending on what inspires you that day.

Find what works for you. Telling yourself a positive story with affirmations, verbal or written, is a great brain-training activity.

I've also realised that I have a much better day when I turn over affirmation cards at the start of the day (watch this space – 'OMG I Am Fabulous' Affirmation Cards coming soon – shameless plug!)

They are like a little whisper of encouragement from whoever or whatever you believe to be supporting you such as the Universe, Spirit guides, or God for example.

They don't take any real thought power, and so are like an effortless message. But it's one that you can interpret in any way you see fit. There is no right or wrong way, and I take comfort in this, like a little hug, smile and nudge forward.

I suppose this is just like reading a horoscope. Or asking a Magic 8 ball to help you make a decision.

These are all tools that we can use that provide a little safety net, helping us look for universal synchronicities and perhaps present some answers or direction.

Tune in to what is meaningful for you. What brings you comfort and you can connect with.

**Breathing**

I've been working on my breathing for some time. First it was for running, then yoga, and more recently hypnobirthing when I was preparing for the birth of Freddy. Both physically and mentally this has helped me so much.

With January, the New Year's resolutions arrived (let's see if we achieve them eh!), and I started listening to guided meditations. There are thousands online. Or pick an app for your phone. These are so accessible and so incredibly beneficial I can't quite explain it.

I still feel pretty new to meditation, and it can take a bit of getting used to. But actually, being able to connect with your mind, body and breath is so peaceful and calming, and also really powerful.

I always find journaling sessions are so much more creative

following meditation.

I'm not gonna pretend I know what happens to make the tears roll down my face on occasion, or how much lighter emotionally I feel.

But what I do know is that the time out from the stresses of the world, allowing us to slow down, and to calm is such an important practice. Increasing mindfulness, focusing on the present moment, connecting and being aware of all that is around and within us, brings a greater level of acceptance and care for ourselves and others. Reducing the level of the stress hormone cortisol in our bodies can have significant health benefits, and there are so many more.

There are many levels to meditation, and it is becoming increasingly popular and a recognised coping mechanism for everyone. From people in high-powered jobs, to those who are more spiritual. I can't yet explain it scientifically, but I'm defo sticking with it! And if you haven't done it, I'd suggest giving it a go.

If you want to rouse some emotions try Tony Robbins 'Priming' on YouTube – wow!

Learning about the Chakras in more depth is certainly on my to-do list as well. Having that awareness of the balance required with all of these energy points within your body, and how any blockages can affect certain elements of our lives, physically and/or emotionally is a real eye-opener. Meditation can help to achieve that alignment.

**Self-care**

All of the above activities are acts of self-care don't you agree? I know I've already mentioned it, but here is a bit more on the subject as I'm really passionate about it.

What even is self-care? It's doing things for ourselves which make us feel good. It's making conscious decisions to take care of our minds and bodies, therefore mentally, emotionally and physically. It's also considering the social and spiritual connections we have with others and ourselves.

In general, we can think of it as a healthy lifestyle and making decisions now that make us feel good within, that serve us well and also that our future-self will thank us for.

It is simple, but it can be so much deeper than this. And there is no 'one-size fits all' self-care plan. Each persons' can be unique to them, because we are all individual.

A concern I have is that some women believe they "don't

have time for self-care". This belief may be seen to be true, however is it? The detriment is that this creates a barrier and puts distance between thinking about doing something, and actually doing it.

I want to highlight that most of us do DO some kind of self-care, but we don't recognise it. Perhaps cos we are so busy and on auto-pilot. However, when we do become more mindful, more aware and recognise that we are giving ourselves some time to focus on what makes us happy, and remove any guilt, we develop a deeper connection with ourselves.

We start to believe that we are worthy of this focus on ourselves, and the self-love becomes real. And from this place of compassion for our own well-being, amazing things can happen.

I've never loved myself more than I do now, and it is special. I feel a sense of calm and peace too.

Self-care shouldn't be thought of as a luxury, but instead essential. You are worth it!

## Mel's Mantra:
## Taking Ownership for your life, inspires Motivation to Go for it!

Reflection time: GETTING STARTED

How am I going to find the time to start to make changes? (Download the Six Steps to Self-Care Guide & Daily Planner for help with this part, link at the back)

Future thinking: What do I want include in my self-care routine?

Mental:

Emotional:

Physical:

Social:

Spiritual:

Future thinking: What do I want to work on to be a better version of me?

Chapter Four

# Feel the Feelings

*"Happiness is a journey, not a destination."* - Alfred D Souza

When we become aware of the **F**eelings associated with the **A**ctions we take and the things we experience, this can help us to take inspired action in the right direction.

**The Comfort Zone**

Many people talk about the comfort zone as an area which we are comfortable within.

Doing things that require extra effort where something may be new territory can be quite scary.

The fear that we have for taking action outside of the place we feel most comfortable is usually concerning other people's perception of us, rather than a physical fear. Unless we take my skydive as an example!

When you get to the space that you have found what's missing (you might be starting to get there) in order to bring that situation to reality, you're going to need to take action. Goal setting is all about doing just that.

Writing the target down on paper is so powerful. But sometimes we don't know where to start. Perhaps your vision seems so far away it's unrealistic. But if it's been done before it can be done again. You just need to find a way. And start with small steps in the right direction.

A consideration to actually put that foot forward is an indication that deep down we do have a desire to move in that direction. The resistance arrives as it's a brand-new thing. So may take that extra bit of effort, confidence, positive self-talk and bravery to push through the barrier.

Very often those things simply won't be in place because what we are about to do is brand new to us. However once attempted, and once that adrenaline rush is over, we can reflect on the outcome, which very often helps to build up the confidence, bravery and PMA surrounding the task. And next time the fearometer isn't cranked up quite as high.

**Fear Vs Discomfort**

Facing something new is often uncomfortable, and really that's what we are feeling. It's not fear, it's actually discomfort.

*'Feel The Fear and Do It Anyway'* by Susan Jeffers helped me push through my own resistance when I was going through a transitional time back in 2011. My Taid (Welsh for Grandfather) had just passed away in front of my eyes, we were preparing to commence our first cycle of IVF and I'd been successful in securing an interview for a promotion at the bank.

Overwhelm consumed me. There was too much going on. But somehow the words Jeffers shared gave me courage to face it all with a positive attitude and muster up the self-belief that I could do this. And I did, and my promotion followed.

Our first fertility injection commenced the same day Prince William & Kate were married, 29th April 2011. Just gone ten years.

We approached every step of the fertility journey batting away the fear, and instead focusing on the positives. Visualising our baby in our arms. Six and a half weeks later we heard the words "You're pregnant!" and our world was filled with delight.

We believed it wholeheartedly, and it happened. There's the LOA again! Wink wink!

**Self-limiting Beliefs**

Now that lot might sound a bit woo-woo, but I 100% believe that "thoughts become things" like The Secret says. So overlay that with the task of goal setting and realise that if you start off in a zone of dis-belief about achieving your goals, you're probably not gonna do it.

This is where PMA (positive mental attitude) is defo required, and positive affirmations. Of course, there are lots of goal setting models to follow to help us, SO MANY! So why don't I add another to the list... (you'll see that in the next chapter).

Our subconscious mind holds on to limiting beliefs that have developed over the years, probably from teenager, if not younger, into early adulthood.

The feelings of "I can't do this" creep in, which arrive from lack of self-belief. But this is where personal development and self-discovery takes over and helps you overcome those thoughts.

When you start to invest in yourself, reading great books, listening to podcasts, connecting with empowering inspirational people, the doubt starts to fade away.

You start to realise your potential. You hear from normal people who have achieved extraordinary things. And more often than not, their focus is on other people, whether its service or product-led, **helping others** becomes their purpose.

That's where I've found myself too.

Realising that feeling fulfilled is a reward in itself. And even better if you can make a career out of what truly lights you up and make you feel your **most fabulous!** Why bloody not pursue this path eh!

**Mindfulness**

I've already touched on this in the previous chapter, but mindfulness has brought a sense of calm to me.

Awareness of the smallest things surrounding me and tapping into my senses more.

As I type this now, I have a buzzing in my ear. Which dependent on what you believe or what you've read, it could be a sign from the universe that I'm on the right path (check out Gabby Bernstein's book 'The Universe has your back').

It's brought me greater appreciation of people, places, objects, and life in general. I also believe mindfulness helps to step away from judgemental viewing of situations and observe things as they are. Almost like you're on the outside looking in and can then consider what's happening with more compassion and understanding. It feels good.

One of the things I have found during these past few months of focusing a lot more on me, and what I truly want, is that I've grown to love myself more. A lot more. I've become a lot more aware of who I am, and what my values are. And with this, I believe brings an increased level of self-belief and self-worth.

A self-confessed self-development junkie, (how many times do I say 'self' in this chapter by the way?! But that is what we are focusing on after all) I'm aiming to point you in the direction of the self-help, self-development sources that have worked for me.

Hopefully the short time it takes you to read or listen to this will be a time-saver in the long run as it will be helping you to do some self-discovery. As well as direct you towards game-changing books, ideas and self-care practices that may also help you to find what you want from life.

## Mel's Mantra:
## **O**neness encourages positive **M**indset, and with this begins **G**oal Getting

Reflection time: FEELINGS

At first thought, what do I want to achieve now? What is stopping me?

A Guide to Being OMG Fabulous

Future thinking: What is most important to me in terms of feelings? How do I want to feel?

## Chapter Five

# Action Taking

This book is 'A Guide to Being OMG Fabulous'. So, its purpose is not to teach you all strategies, but to introduce another viewpoint. Something which may inspire you and show you that change is possible for absolutely ANYONE who wants it!

I've already mentioned how I've overlayed OMGFAB onto my morning routine, sorry *ritual*! But that wasn't the original intention of this book. It's just a massive coincide and perhaps another universal synchronicity! (I bloody love it!)

The next part shows you the six key things that have impacted my life and the lives of those I work with. By focusing on these aspects, change happens, that's how it works.

When thinking about making changes, try to consider this...

<u>O – Ownership</u>     It's down to YOU, no one else. Think OMG! (more to follow)

<u>M – Mindset</u>      Your internal dialogue will impact the decisions you make and actions you take, so be kind to yourself always, with positive talk and encouraging affirmations. Mindset also impacts Motivation

<u>G – Goal setting</u>   Be clear on 'what' exactly it is that you want to achieve and think about 'how' creatively.

Visualise the outcome, but do not become transfixed on it. Instead enjoy the journey!

(There is also OMGFAB for specific Goals next)

F – Feelings

Be mindful. Think about how you feel at EVERY step, take a memory picture to reflect on and to spur you on when you need it, helping you to do more of the good stuff

A – Action

Take action, explore opportunities, learn from them and step outside the comfort zone #justdoit

B – Belief

Practice means progress (thank you Lisa Walsh). Push through barriers to prove to yourself that YOU CAN and YOU WILL achieve what you truly desire. Be aware of your areas of vulnerability and doubt, then find a strategy for coping and overcoming this. Celebrate achievements along the way, you deserve it

These headlines are what have worked for me in stepping

forward and I hope they can for you to, with whatever changes you want to make. They can be overlayed across anything. Health improvements, personal development, career, habit formation. Try it!

Now here is a practical and simple tool, specifically for GOAL SETTING.

I'm sure you'll have heard of many goal-setting models which have been put together to increase the chances of success. So here is my simple version which aligns to the OMGFAB message and can be used with a single goal in mind.

**Ownership** – Be accountable, write it down, tell someone

**Motivation** – Why are you doing it? Keep asking yourself 'why' until you can go no further

**Goal** – What is it that you actually want to do? And by when? Put a date on it!

**Feelings** – Visualise how will you feel during and after you've achieved the goal? Also how you feel as part of the process, keep tapping in to this along the way

**Assessment** – Review throughout and ongoing, what have you learned from this process

**Belief** – Celebrate your achievements - the success and the learning

So why not give it a go. Grab a pen and piece of paper and write down the six headings.

Here is my EXAMPLE:

**Ownership** – *I'm going to tell my Facebook group members Feel Fab OMG.*

**Motivation** – *I have spent so many hours figuring out what works for me, reading different books, listening to training, learning. If this can help one person get there faster and inspire them to believe that change is possible, then it will all be worth it. I love helping others & want to make a positive difference to everyone I encounter, helping women feel fab on the inside & out is my mission. I want to take them from thinking about it, to doing it.*

**Goal** – *Complete my publishing course and publish my book before my 40<sup>th</sup> birthday (Jan '22). Helping hundreds of women to make positive changes that help them to feel more fulfilled.*

**Feelings** – *Accomplished and satisfied that I have done what I said I was going to do. Helping women and inspiring change in*

*those who want to change is what really lights me up. Knowing I've played a little part will be the biggest reward for me, and I will feel honoured to have helped.*

**Assessment** – *I procrastinate a lot, but have overcome so many personal barriers. Learning to self-publish means I will be able to help others who want to publish in the future too. I feel proud of myself of how far I've come to this point.*

**Belief** – *As I'm writing this I have almost done it!....* more to be completed in this space!

I hope my example shows you that goal setting does not need to be scary or complicated.

Achieving goals is another story, because that is down to us and taking ACTION. And often we can get in our own way.

If we overlay every decision we make with a long-term thinking approach, then we can start to make better decisions in so many areas of our lives. We can start to identify the difference between the instant gratification moments, that seem harmless but actually push us further away from our goals.

Think OMG! What is this?

**O**wn

**M**y

**G**oals

Those moments of self-sabotage, when you've been doing so well working towards a specific goal and you find yourself in a moment of weakness...

### Think OMG!

### Shout OMG!

Either silently in your mind, or maybe verbally to prove a point! But use this as a distraction tool.

OK it sounds easier than it is, I get this. But it works! Give it a whirl (and don't forget to tag me on your socials when you do it pretty please!)

The first step is awareness, which of course is everything, as we've already discussed that we do things subconsciously.

But by taking OWNERSHIP and becoming more aware of all ACTIONS taken, you can OWN YOUR GOALs and determine your own success in achieving them.

For example, if your goal is to lose weight to feel better in your clothes, and improve your health, that is fab. But go one step deeper with the goal setting, ask yourself "WHY?" again. OK, perhaps its so that you are here on planet earth a bit longer, and can enjoy your later years with your family as you are reducing the risk of developing diseases later in life. Those that can be life-limiting such as heart disease, diabetes or dementia. Wow that got deep didn't it? But it's fact. You need to go deep in order to take notice.

For years I yo-yo dieted. I've tried so many different programmes and potions in the past. But it was always about how I looked externally. I wasn't trying to lose weight for health benefits. And I think that's why it always seemed a struggle in the past.

However, becoming a Dementia Friend, and then a Dementia Friend Champion so that I could deliver the training too, I became more interested in understanding dementia. A few more courses later and I began to recognise that we can actually reduce our risk of developing this disease. What an eye opener.

All of a sudden, I connected my reasons for wanting to maintain a healthy weight to the long-term health benefits, and it altered my decision making with food. Instead making more mindful food choices today, so that I can do as much as possible to live a long and healthy life, and not become a burden to my family. The thought of them being upset because of me breaks my heart.

My aim is to be here **as the best version of myself** for as long as possible.

Really delve deeper with your goal setting and overlay the long-term benefits or outcomes of the goals, and that will help you make better choices and connect with your goal(s).

If weight management is one, I'm not saying you have to cut out all treats and totally change your diet as that's a lot to ask.

But if you're pondering whether to get the take-away tonight as you've "done really well" with healthy eating, so it'll be a nice "reward" hmmmm?! Instead, you can choose to continue the streak you're on, and opt for a healthier option, so you don't have to start all over again.

Think of the instant benefit today, but also positive actions for the future you that you're bringing into existence.

Close your eyes and allow yourself to daydream about what

life will be like with your goal(s) achieved.

Visualise your future self, what you are doing and how you are feeling. Fully immerse yourself in that scenario so much so that it's as though you are sat there right now. You need to replay these positive images over and over to bring it to life.

When you can get lost in these thoughts it's so powerful, connecting your emotions and senses to this moment in time, smell, see, feel your surroundings as though it's really real. Your belief in this scenario will determine your level of motivation in taking action.

If you don't believe it, you won't achieve it. Sorry to be blunt, but that's just the way it is. So, you might need to work on those limiting beliefs, and whatever it is that's standing in your way. *'Fearless & Fabulous'* by Cara Alwill Leyba is a great book for delving deeper to tackling those blockers.

It is really important to get a balance between your long-term vision and the here and now.

Linking small tangible everyday goals to your long-term vision is essential for moving the needle closer to where you want to be. So if it's only one thing you accomplish on any given day, that should be celebrated as it's another step closer.

Enjoy this present moment, as this is part of the process. Don't wish your life away or complain about your life today. Display and live with an attitude of gratitude and attract more great things into your life (there's the LOA again!)

Your vibes are a magnet. Keep them high.

There is certainly no point or value in comparing your life now to how it used to be, as that is in the past, and that's where it will stay.

Every single thing that you've experienced in your life so far has made you the person you are today. Some of those may be good, some bad, but regardless they have made you YOU!

***"Every experience in your life is a perfect opportunity to know yourself at a deeper level."*** Gray, 'Raise Your Vibration'.

And you are here right now, reading this book, developing yourself and maybe starting to look at life a little differently.

You are exactly where you need to be.

Plan tomorrow today. This sounds very short term doesn't it. This goes back to the O for Organisation in the morning ritual I do, it actually starts the night before.

If you can sit down each evening and think of one action you can plan for tomorrow that will move you closer towards your goals then this will help you to avoid procrastination.

The fact you have planned it means you have thought about it, and without realising you allow your mind to visualise yourself doing that task, whatever it is, which is a productive thought.

When you become conscious of this, picture yourself doing it with ease.

Talk to yourself positively, and rewire your brain so that those neural pathways are programmed with a positive mental "can-do" attitude.

If it's typically negative thoughts in your mind, then this is going to take some time and some work. But by now, hopefully you've started to think about this through the eyes of a person who says, *'I can do this'*.

## Mel's Mantra:
## <u>O</u>wn <u>M</u>y <u>G</u>oals

Reflection time: ACTION

How can I adopt long-term thinking into my everyday life?

Reflection time: What do I want to change about my life?

Future thinking: What action(s) can I take immediately to progress towards my goal(s)?

## Chapter Six

# Belief

LET'S GO! BOOM! WAHOOOOO! You feel all fired up, don't you?! I'm hoping YES! Please!

Our motivation levels can feel so sparked up at times, and we are raring to go. It's awesome! And then something happens. A mood-hoover of a friend or family member overlays their existing fears of THEIR OWN limiting beliefs they have (of themselves) on to us! And we listen to their 'words of wisdom', which are often defo not words of wisdom at all. WTF?! Why do we do that?

And why do we take advice from people who often aren't happy in their own space? It's easier to live in a place of fear. It's submissive, it doesn't require any energy, in fact it drains our energy.

Whereas if we push ourselves into the growth space, where we are changing, and developing, this takes effort. Effort implies a use of energy, which when exhausted, implies tiredness. And that is when we HAVE to use our internal fuel (our motivation) to drive us forward. By filling our lives with things that make us feel fab it gives us energy daily, and there are so many studies which now prove that happiness keeps us healthy too.

Another reason why self-care is essential!

That's why is it SO important to become connected to your 'WHY'. Your purpose. Your reason for doing all this, for considering making adjustments. In many cases the changes, I assume, will positively impact your overall well-being. It doesn't make sense to consider changes that will sabotage you or cause you any detriment does it? But aside from your well-being and fulfilment, it may also impact other things or people.

What is your 'why'?

I kept playing around with which part of the book this topic should appear. I had it at the start, and then at the goal setting section. And even though YOUR MOTIVATOR is quite possibly the most important factor in you deciding to become your own version of OMG Fabulous, I decided that it would feature in the last chapter. Because at the end of the day, whenever you feel at the end of your tether and like giving up, you need that reminder for WHY you are doing what you do… your WHY!

This can be your fuel. This can be your energy. This can be your strength when things become tough and you're feeling far from fabulous.

You remember your WHY and it encourages you to take inspired action in the direction of your goals.

This is the direction you need to go in, and the one where the magic will happen. If you do nothing, then nothing will change. Fact.


I've heard so much about 'Imposter Syndrome' over the last few months. And I can totally relate. Can you? When you think about your desires and then question yourself.

I've been asking myself questions like:

"Who am I to write a book?"

"Why would anyone care what I have to say?"

"Will anyone even want to read it?"

It's been written for months, and I, for so long came up with the excuse of being stuck in my publishing course, so not able to learn how to format it as paperback (I can hear myself now and am rolling my eyes at myself). I couldn't get the page numbering right, the formatting was off, my website isn't ready etc. But I've gone with "progress over perfection", and just done it!

You're possibly laughing now as I've said this to so many people, you've likely heard me say it. Or perhaps this resonates with something you've personally experienced.

I just wanted to acknowledge that I believe it is normal, and I am living proof of procrastination at its best!

We often go through a time of comparison to others, and tell ourselves that we can't possibly do what the other person has done, because of x, y, and z reasons. Talking ourselves out of our greatness. But in reality, we should use others as our inspiration to show us it's been done before, so can be done again!

Maybe even just giving ourselves the label of being stuck in 'imposter syndrome' is another excuse. Just a delay tactic, as we are getting close, and its self-preservation.

We are protecting ourselves from the possibility of failure or ridicule. When realistically if we just did the thing we want to do, with conviction, then people who love and care for us will support us and will all come round to our way of thinking. And who knows maybe they will start to overcome their own limiting beliefs too.

Imagine that! Inspiring others… that's all I want to do. To show that change is possible if it's what *you want*.

That change can be in any capacity, great or small, regardless, the change CAN make a difference, and can help you to be YOUR version of OMG Fabulous.

You just need to **choose** to do it!

**Accountability**

I'm gonna throw another suggestion in… Be Brave!

Why not tell someone what you want to do? Share your feelings, thoughts, desires, goals or plan.

You may need to choose wisely who you decide to tell, as those mood-hoovers can easily pull the carpet out from under you or take the wind out of your sails. So, if you're nervous it may be an idea to look for people to connect with to share your ideas with.

A safe space filled with like-minded people who are on a similar path to you. Who are making changes whether they be health, mind, or career. Whatever the change there is a group for everything on the socials.

Reach out to me, and I'll share some amazing people and places that have helped me find my self-belief so far on my journey.

When you are ready say it out loud and make it real. Even if you practice to yourself in the mirror (I talk to myself a lot in the mirror by the way, especially before I deliver any training) as things sound different out loud. Verbalising information allows us to process it differently too.

Another tip is to record yourself on your phone. Have a chat with yourself and watch it back. I can almost guarantee you will cringe at the start, but the more you do it, the more confident you will become about the change you want to make, and whether it feels aligned to you.

For so many of us, we hold things in our mind or visions, but are afraid to make the commitment of saying them out loud. Because it makes it real. However, once you do, and say it to others you make yourself accountable.

Many of us hold integrity as a value. Meaning we hold strong moral principles, and we want to **do what we say we are going to do**. Basically, with integrity in mind you are committing to yourself and others that you are going to take action.

Once we say it out loud, and connect it to our WHY, we set our intentions, interlinking Feelings and Actions to demonstrate that we do have self-Belief. And we can and will do this! FAB! FAB! FAB!

### Mel's Mantra:

**Openheartedly Make my Gift of life count. I am here for a reason!**

Reflection time: BELIEVE

What is my WHY?

## Conclusion

# What Next

My hope is that by now you feel some kind of spark in you with a drive to do something to help you find the fulfilment you're looking for.

Hopefully I've got my point across about how important it is to realise that your happiness won't come purely from achieving your goals. It is actually part of the process of today.

Life is a journey! (My next tattoo)

From experience I can share that when you start to enjoy the **here and now**, and live for the moment, having faith that what is meant to be will be and you are worthy of the life you want to live, everything becomes a whole lot more peaceful.

What are you taking from this read…?

Take what you will, after all, how qualified am I to even share this information?

Hang on, time for me to reframe that thought…Here it goes; I was a person who wanted more from life, and **I am now** doing more with my life that makes ME feel fulfilled. It gives me more purpose and I feel passionate about it.

**I am feeling OMG Fabulous!**

This is what we need to do.

Overcome our self-doubt, our own barriers, our own limiting beliefs that halt us like a deer in headlights and stop us from moving forward.

Why should I keep my mouth closed and not share what I

want to say?

Surely, I have a duty of care to share what's inside of me if it's going to help others? If I kept it to myself that would be selfish, and I would feel crap. Lose:lose! Simple as that really isn't it.

If any of the information that I have shared with you can give you a kickstart to take action, then I know my time and effort in writing my first self-published book has been well spent.

I can't declare that I have letters after my name, a global six or seven figure business, and client testimonials coming out of my ears…yet!

But I can show you that in January 2021 I had a vision. That was to write a book before I turn 40. And here I am, I've written it. So, I got shit done! I found a way make it happen, despite being time poor and with a low budget. And by proving this to myself I know it's just the start of things to come.

***"Whatever the mind can conceive and believe, the mind can achieve."*** Napoleon Hill

On reflection I am a wife, mother and grandmother whose circumstances changed, and my old way of life just didn't fit for me anymore. And actually, through some self-discovery activities I've become clearer on what makes me feel fab, and realised that I've a lot to give to this world on a wider scale.

I've known this for a while, but I didn't quite know how to take it forward.

I found my passion in people development and coaching during my twelve-year corporate career.

Since taking my leap of faith into the self-employed space, I have learned new skills and worked with more women on a one-to-one basis.

Having experienced different challenges and learning more about myself than ever before...

From the self-doubt brought by feeling vulnerable having left a four-figure weekly role, to the insecurity and uncertainty of self-employment. And the helplessness of taking time off work and not being paid. Throw a pandemic in the mix, as well as maternity leave…jeepers! Financial pressure overload.

To then feeling the empowerment inspiring myself and

following my heart. And discovering the difference I'm making to other women, by introducing them to things that can help them FEEL FAB on the inside and out!

Finding other opportunities and income streams that can pay residually or passively and allow for fulfilling my role as a parent and grandparent, without sacrificing family time. And get paid for doing what lights me up inside – win:win!

Being a cheerleader for others, helping women to discover their fabulousness.

Also sharing my journey and how I've personally developed and adapted to change or difficult times. I know I have time-served experience to offer and in the main I've kept a smile on my face.

Sometimes that smile was hard work, and I wasn't feeling it inside. No one is indestructible. We are all human. So, keeping it real is key. Authenticity is essential.

Burn out is inevitable if we don't keep things balanced and allow ourselves time-out every now and again. I've learned this the hard way.

Keeping in-check with ourselves needs to be on the self-care agenda, and it's helped me to develop and learn coping strategies which I can share with others, to help them avoid mistakes I have made.

But right now, the happiness is real, it is radiating. And since I've taken the time to focus on ME, find fulfilment, and feel OMG FAB, it doesn't feel like it's going to stop.

I describe myself as an 'open book' and have been told on numerous occasions that I should write one, and how my sharing our fertility journey and other life lessons has helped others. And now as you come to end this one, I hope it has helped you! xxx

**"We don't quit. I don't quit. Let's seize this moment."** – Barack Obama

By taking little baby steps towards where we want to be, putting ourselves out there in that space a little more, we get closer to the reality of what might be if we just keep on going and don't give up.

Quitting is the only way to fail, everything else is part of the learning journey.

It may be a scary rollercoaster at times, but guess what, you can't get off mid-ride, you've got to wait until the end. Imagine the thrill of it when you realise you've conquered that ride, you stuck it out, and you made it – safe and sound!

I've been a stepmother for almost 20 years, that's basically half my life. And so very grateful and blessed with the extended family I have. Motherhood started with these two beautiful humans. I adore them. As well as Les (Joe & Em's Mum) who is like a sister to me. Her family are incredible. I've always felt welcome. It's special, and we are very aware we are in the minority situation where ex and current wife can be so close. This is our choice, and it's so bloody lovely!

A quarter of my life ago I went through the scariest thing with the biggest responsibility I've ever encountered. Bringing our daughter into this world. Surrounded with love, support and guidance from so many people in my life. So very fortunate, and still extremely grateful.

How frickin' mind blowing are our bodies by the way? From conception, whether it being natural or assisted like ours, to growing a little human inside of us, then somehow getting it out! Whether natural childbirth or through the sunroof, it blows my mind when I think about it for too long. And all those incredible doctors and nurses who have trained tirelessly to keep us and our broods safe. I am truly grateful.

I realise now after giving birth to our second miracle that anything is possible – and I can do anything!

Being a new Mummy again has been MY trigger. And I know I will impact their (my kids) future with every decision I make. And I CAN do this so positively, yes me, Mummy. I don't want our children to have to go through hard times or worry about how they're going to have to pay for things.

I want to discover better ways to for us to live that makes us happy and reduces stress. I want to inspire our children, and grandchildren and anyone else who wants to listen. And emphasize that it's not necessary to conform to the stereotypical way of life.

We've all heard it… go to school, get good grades, go to university, get a good job, work until you're well into your 60s.

I am not knocking anyone who has done this of course. I have so many friends and family on this path, and I respect their decisions, and love their journeys and seeing their happiness.

Plus, I am totally inspired and in awe of my amazing parents who have just recently retired both in their 60s. Having had successful careers and now in a comfortable position. They are both well respected and people who make a difference for absolutely no benefit of their own. They give so much of themselves with no expectation of return. I love their values. They are truly incredible!

I accept that things very frequently don't follow the *ideal* or *stereotypical path*. And many of us find ourselves in very different circumstances, but still trying to make an impact. Wanting to make a positive difference to others, to the wider community, to the world. And guess what happens as a result for anyone who puts themselves out there on the pursuit of helping others... a chance of more fulfilment, greater happiness, more meaningful relationships. Those closest to us also benefit from our elevated feelings of self-worth and purpose. If we don't pursue the path we are drawn to, we risk missing out on all that fabulous stuff. Now that would be a tragedy.

Maybe if I had made different choices at an earlier age, I would have found fulfilment sooner.

And perhaps I would have been in a position where I was confident in my plan for retirement. But there is no point in the shoulda, woulda, couldas. We are talking about where we are at now. And where I am at now is HERE. Where you are at now is HERE! Life is a journey.

I actually wish I had completed my French and Spanish degree. Not just because I want to be fluent in those languages, but because I hate not following things through to completion. Typical Capricorn! So, to drop out of Uni in my second year, as I was scared to move abroad for a year, insecure in my new relationship with Heath almost 20 years ago. I chose to stay. I chose a new path.

For so long felt like there was a big sign flashing at me in neon lighting. 'FAILURE! FAILURE!'. Then when I heard Gray say ***"No external achievement will ever determine how amazing you are. And it wants you to trust that it's always working for your greatest good."***

I realised that I wasn't meant to complete that degree, and IT aka 'the universe' had other plans for me. Maybe I will get a cap and gown one day, we will see. But that will not define me.

For now, I will continue to share my story of how, in my 39th year, I had a vision of our future life, of the service I can provide to other women helping them **"Feel FAB on the inside and out"**.

And guess what, it might have taken 39 years, but I've actually now found what I want to do now that I'm grown up. I've figured out that I can help others who feel a bit flat or stuck, by showing them (or you) it's possible to find a way to become unstuck, to find hope and excitement. To go from feeling flat to FAB!

And part of it has involved me writing a book as a starter, and here it is.

OMG I've done it! *OMG I feel Fabulous!*


It may only be a short transcript, but I hope it adds some value to your life. Perhaps it's inspired you to read another motivational self-help book. Maybe the journaling aspect with the tasks has encouraged you to start scribing daily to get your thoughts on to paper.

Whether this gives you some ideas to explore, or you just

start to connect with yourself on a deeper level, it's still a positive step forward. When it comes to change, I truly believe that it's a good thing.

And I also believe that **doing something** is better than nothing.

There is no measure on how big change needs to be. All that matters is that you're doing something for yourself, and can discover what makes you *feel fab*, developing your own self-care requirements. And that you love yourself more as a result.

Whatever you've taken from this, I would love to know if this has sparked something in you. Please leave me a review wherever you can. Tag me on the socials (see back of book) and if you feel someone else would benefit then please share this with them.

But let's get back to the most important thing, YOU!

This is about what is important to you. So here is my final question…

Future thinking: BEING OMG FABULOUS

What is your version of OMG Fabulous? And what are you going to do next?

## Acknowledgments

To my husband Heath, thank you for telling me to "JUST DO IT!" Looks like I listened, and here I am. I hope this is the start of things to come, as a publisher and author I will help others and make a difference to their lives. Which in turn will make a difference to ours. I love you, and will forever be yours.

To our children Joe & wife Demi, Emma, Amelia and Freddy, and our grandkids Harley and Jaxson, thank you for being my driver. I hope that I will make you proud. You are my 'why'. I love you all, and hope that I can inspire you to follow your hearts.

To my parents, Steven & Gaynor, you are amazing. I have so much to thank you for and can only hope that I can repay you in some way. I am so grateful for the upbringing you provided for Joe and I. Joseph, Rachel, James & Michael I did it! Love you all so much.

To my in-laws Ruth & Johnny, thank you for bringing Heath into the world, and for all of your support for our family. Sending love & good health to you both always.

To my besties, Nisha, Kaz, Lesley and Charlotte. Your vibe attracts your tribe they say, and I have the best tribe! Thank you all for your support, I value and cherish each of your friendships individually and more than I can describe. I love you all.

Soooooooo many amazing friends, I am so very fortunate to be surrounded by such kindness and compassion, support and smiles. Vanessa, Kerry, Katie, Claire, Esther, Rachael, Donna, Cheryl, Lindi, Fiona...the list goes on. There are SO many more I'd love to mention, but it would be endless. I'm confident you know who you are, and I am so grateful that you are part of my life.

I have to give Jody Murphy (of Skin You Will Love Academy) a shout out for helping me with my rebrand from The Lash Expert to OMG Melanie Gizzi a few years back with my beauty business. As well as your friendship & support always.

The one and only Branding Fairy Godmother Jojo Smith. I don't think you realise the impact you've had to my life.. I believe the Universe brought you and CreativSAS into my Facebook newsfeed for a reason. You bring joy to every communication we have; you inspire me to take action. Although I know you say you just guided me to see it, you gave me OMG Fabulous! I'm so thankful that you are helping me to find my SAS – bloody love you and am so grateful for you!

Imagine having royalty in your entourage. Well, I have The Queen Bee Dani Wallace. Working with you helped me to see the life experience I have to bring to the table, and that I can share it for the benefit of others. This book was originally called "A Quick Guide to Finding Fulfillment" and only 5K words, until you inspired me to create a signature system and put my unique stamp on it as OMG Fabulous. I aspire to be able to share my message, just as you do yours. You're awesome, thank you! I'm so excited for the next Bee Inspired!

Then from Dani's Hive has born another connection with The Feminine Energy Guide herself, Niki Kinsella. There was a reason I was dilly dallying with publishing this. I now know that I needed Niki in my life to help me discover my own blocks and push through my barriers. You have helped me to understand the reasons why I do some of the things I do. Our relationship is still quite new, but I feel I've known you forever, and I'm super excited of what else will be uncovered. Thank you so much.

Louisa Herridge of Mama's Ignited has also provided great levels of support and encouragement at the start of me doing this book. Thank you for showing me that it's ok to have similar messaging as women in business – we all deliver it in our own way, and attract the right people to us.

To my clients and customers, thank you for all your continued support over the years. I love the community we have created on Facebook **Feel Fab OMG**, and hope the positive, supportive space we hold continues to flourish.

The inspirational people in my life, there are many. I look up to business builders, coaches, entrepreneurs, authors, and take guidance from your actions and words.

*If it's been done before it can be done again!*

**About Mel**

Melanie Gizzi, founder of OMG Fabulous, is on a mission to help women FEEL FAB on the inside and out! A twelve-year corporate background led Mel to quickly find her passion in helping others to develop. Nothing lights her up more than seeing others have an OMG moment! Mel's dedication to help others become better versions of themselves in the workplace led to many awards during her career.

Significantly, Mel and husband Heath discovered it was unlikely they would conceive naturally. They have shared their fertility journey openly to help others, and whilst Mel says this was her "therapy", she also realised how sharing truly is caring, and self-care is essential for dealing with challenging times.

Their first child Amelia was born via IVF. However, subsequent attempts were unsuccessful, yet they remained positive.

A leap of faith to allow for more family time saw Melanie exit the corporate world. Now the owner of beauty business OMG (Oh Melanie Gizzi), which naturally expanded to focus on overall wellbeing, she is also a certified Life Coach with an Award in Education & Training.

Amongst her community she is known for self-care, positivity and mindset focus. The news of a natural pregnancy further cemented her belief in the law of attraction, spirituality and all things miraculous! And defying the odds, Freddy was born at the start of the pandemic.

An introducer to ideas or concepts perhaps never explored, Mel's desire is to help women to feel safe to take steps forward into unknown territory. So that they can find their fabulousness. As an **O**rganisation & **M**otivation **G**uide, she offers inspiration to her clients through demonstrating how to prioritise self-care; introduce purposeful changes; get things done; stay organised and remain self-motivated, even in today's busy world.

A 5am riser, she spends child-free mornings completing a self-care ritual, including yoga or running when possible. Wind-down time often involves cuddles with Hubby, personal development or a good book! Any spare time is spent with the whole brood, including her grown stepchildren Emma, and Joe, with his wife Demi, and two grandchildren Harley and Jaxson (Nana Wednesdays rule!)

## Connect with Mel:

Linktree (Every important link is on this one - just need to learn how to build my website next!): https://linktr.ee/omgfabulous

Free Facebook Group:
https://www.facebook.com/groups/FeelFabOMG

Instagram: https://Instagram.com/melgizzi @melgizzi

LinkedIn: https://www.linkedin.com/in/melanie-gizzi-347b4b30/

Six Steps to Self-Care Guide & Free Daily Planner

https://www.subscribepage.com/six-steps-to-self-care

## Resources

Byrne, R. (2006). *The Secret* (10th Anniversary ed.). Atria Books/Beyond Words.

Byrne, R. (2010). *The Power (The Secret)* (1st ed.). Atria Books.

Byrne, R. (2012). *The Magic (Secret (Rhonda Byrne))* (Illustrated ed.). Atria Books.

Elrod, H. (2021). *The Miracle Morning: The 6 Habits that Will Transform Your Life Before 8 a.m.* John Murray Learning.

Frances, A., & Alwill, C. (2021). *Rich As F\*ck: More Money Than You Know What to Do With*. Amanda Frances Inc.

Gray, K. (2016). *Raise Your Vibration: 111 Practices to Increase Your Spiritual Connection* (1st ed.). Hay House Inc.

*Feel The Fear And Do It Anyway: How to Turn Your Fear and Indecision into Confidence and Action by Susan Jeffers (4-Jan-2007) Paperback.* (2021). Vermilion; 20Anniversary Ed edition (4 Jan. 2007).

Leyba, A. C. (2014). *Fearless & Fabulous: 10 Powerful Strategies for Getting Anything You Want in Life*. Passionista Publishing.

**Praise for the Author**

"I just want to say how grateful I am to be part of your journey in OMG fabulous.

I went through incredible trauma some months ago, and life was pretty crap, I seen no light at the end of the tunnel. I felt I had lost myself. Both myself and my daughter were struggling, and I found it so hard to apply myself to be a Mum and to get on with normal daily routine.

A week post event you added me to your group, which gave me inspiration when I needed it the most. Starting by reading your posts etc. I started trying to get myself thinking differently to help myself.

Since being part of the group and reading your book and putting your self-help and wellbeing ideas into practice, I feel so much more calm, and feel I have more inner peace! Before my head would catastrophise my thoughts etc. and I couldn't sleep. Focusing on positivity and gratitude every evening is so positive for me as it means I don't dwell on negative thoughts when the children go to bed! I also get my 8year old daughter involved so that she focuses on positive things, as she has really struggled with being separated from me at night when it's time to go to bed.

I also notice that when she tells me stories about other children in school, I feel myself reiterating the mindfulness and gratitude you practice, to reinforce her maintaining a positive outlook and to grow being a better person.

I think it shows how important self-care is, how much you need grounding to keep you in the here and now. I love how you share your bad days too, you show us it is ok not to be ok, and makes you realise we are not on our own.

We look for love hearts everywhere we go because I want her to know the world is a beautiful place, and now we're starting to look for angel numbers, and what that means.

Honestly we both get so much from it, and I just wanted to thank you ☺ I feel so much more myself and positive about what 2022 has to bring.

You are an amazing person <3 a real true inspiration to women of this generation and the next <3 and keep on with your OMG Fabulous work as you're having such a positive impact on so many women's lives giving such a strong message of female empowerment xx"

*– Cheryl Roberts*


"I just wanted to send you a quick message to say how fab your group is and how much it is motivating me to become a better version of myself. My bestie Cheryl added me to the group before Christmas and I love being part of it. 2 years ago I was doing Habit (HIIT) classes 4 times a week, looked and felt great. Then COVID hit and my motivation has just gone from a hundred to zero. Also "mum guilt" kicked in because I felt that my son has done nothing for a whole year, so I booked him into karate, swimming and Beavers, which has left me with no time for myself.

Seeing you do yoga and exercise at home and look as fab as you do has given me the motivation that I needed. I've downloaded the FitOn app and have started using it this week, have also started journaling my meals and trying to practice mindful eating as opposed to mindless eating. I've also started practicing little things like gratitude, time blocking, journaling, thinking about things that make me happy and most importantly have started making time for myself. I'm just in the middle of reading your book and I think you're a breath of fresh air (note to self – don't read before bed, it's very thought provoking. My head was full of all these ideas in the middle of the night).

Just thought I'd let you know how grateful I am for being part of Feel Fab OMG and how inspirational I find you as a person <3 xx"

- *Gundega Overthrow*

Printed in Great Britain
by Amazon